D1459777

SUPER SMART
INFORMATION
STRATEGIES

# MAKE YOUR POINT: CREATING POWERFUL PRESENTATIONS

by Ann Truesdell

CHERRY LAKE PUBLISHING • ANN ARBOR, MICHIGAN

A NOTE TO PARENTS AND TEACHERS: Please remind your children how to stay safe online before they do the activities in this book.

A NOTE TO KIDS: Always remember your safety comes first!

CHERRY LAKE
Publishing

Published in the United States of America
by Cherry Lake Publishing
Ann Arbor, Michigan
www.cherrylakepublishing.com

Content Adviser: Gail Dickinson, PhD,
Associate Professor, Old Dominion University

Photo Credits: Cover, ©BLD0111798/Media Bakery; page 4, ©Avava/
Dreamstime.com; page 10, "DSC04416" by Barrett.Discovery on Flickr.
com, available under a Creative Commons Attribution license (http://
creativecommons.org/licenses/by/3.0/); page 11, ©Corbis Premium RF/Alamy;
page 12, ©Dmitriy Shironosov/Shutterstock, Inc.; pages 14 and 15, Library
of Congress; page 16, ©Klara Viskova/Shutterstock, Inc.; page 18, ©Goodluz/
Shutterstock, Inc.; page 19, ©Jacek Chabraszewski/Shutterstock, Inc.; page 22,
©netbritish/Shutterstock, Inc.; page 27, ©Myrleen Pearson/Alamy.

Library of Congress Cataloging-in-Publication Data
Truesdell, Ann.
  Make your point : creating powerful presentations / by Ann Truesdell.
       pages cm — (Information explorer)
  Includes bibliographical references and index.
  ISBN 978-1-62431-019-5 (lib. bdg.) — ISBN 978-1-62431-043-0 (pbk.) —
ISBN 978-1-62431-067-6 (e-book)
  1. Public speaking—Juvenile literature. I. Title.
  PN4129.15.T78 2013                                    2012034742
  808.5'1—dc23

Cherry Lake Publishing would like to acknowledge the work of The Partnership
for 21st Century Skills. Please visit www.21stcenturyskills.org for more
information.

Printed in the United States of America
Corporate Graphics Inc.
January 2013
CLSP12

# Table of Contents

# CHAPTER ONE
# Know Your Stuff

Have you ever had the chance to present information to your classmates?

Have you ever sat in class and wished for the opportunity to get up and teach the other students? Someday, your teacher will probably ask you to give an oral presentation in front of the class. That's your chance! An oral presentation is when you speak in front an audience to teach them about a subject.

Oral presentations are different than other types of presentations that you may have done in the past. Many students create posters, **slideshows**, and even short movies as ways of presenting information they have learned. They might put these presentations up in their classrooms or post them online. An oral presentation requires you to speak in front of an audience yourself. Some oral presentations might be recorded on video, but most will be live—just you in front of the class! In a live presentation, there are no do-overs, and you can't go back and edit. That is why it is important to prepare, practice, and provide visuals that help your audience understand your topic.

The first step is to understand your assignment. What does your teacher want you to present about? You will probably need to do some research to learn more about your topic. As you research, make sure you learn the basic facts about your topic, such as who, what, why, where, when, and how. Many teachers call those facts the "five Ws and one H." Look at other facts about your topic that interest you, too, and consider which ones would be most interesting to your audience.

Next, it is time to sort out your information and decide how you will present it to your class. Giving a good presentation is like telling a good story. You should start by introducing your topic, including the people who are involved in your topic and where any events took place. You might introduce

Put It All Together, by Phyllis Cornwall, is a great book to read for more help sorting out all of your information!

something that was a problem and let your audience know you'll be explaining how this problem was solved.

Let's pretend you are presenting about the Wright brothers and their invention of the first powered airplane. You might start by talking about the beach in North Carolina where the brothers tested their plane designs. It's also a good idea to give a little background information on the topic. For example, you might be presenting mostly about the Wright brothers' contributions to flight, but do your classmates know that they were not the first people to build and test aircraft?

Next, you should tell your audience what your presentation is about. You want to present the facts that are most important for them to know. Again, think about presenting like telling a story. Make sure that all of your ideas connect to one another instead of just throwing out random facts. Think about the questions your audience might have, and try to answer those questions before they are even asked. A presentation about airplanes might move past the Wright brothers and into World War I (1914–1918), when airplanes were first tested as weapons. You would probably then move past that into the days of legendary pilot Amelia Earhart and then on to the use of planes in World War II (1939–1945). You could end your "story" by talking about commercial flights that people use for business and travel. You would want to be sure to note how the aircraft changed along the way.

Make sure that the topics in your presentation connect smoothly to one another.

Just like ending a story, you will need to tie up any loose ends or show how the problem was solved. Tell the audience what came next, after the events in your presentation. For example, you might end your airplane presentation by telling how else planes are used today or how today's planes are built. You may want to emphasize the most important three or four facts that you hope your audience will have learned from your presentation.

To get a copy of this activity, visit www.cherrylakepublishing.com/activities.

# TRY THIS!

As you sort through your information and prepare for your presentation, it is usually helpful to create an outline so you can see what you are going to say and when. You might do this on paper or on a computer.

BRAINSTORM

Let's practice outlining a presentation. Think about a topic that you already know a lot about. Maybe you play soccer, or perhaps you are very interested in trains or dogs. Try to brainstorm three main **subtopics** that you would want to speak about in your presentation. What information would fall under each subtopic? Next, begin to organize your information. You might choose to make an outline like the one below:

Main Topic: Adopting a Dog
I. Subtopic: Choosing the Best Dog for
   Your Family
   A. Different breeds and types of dogs
   B. Puppies versus adult dogs
II. Subtopic: Where to Get a Dog
   A. Pet stores
   B. Breeders
   C. Shelters
III. Subtopic: Things to Consider
   Before You Adopt a Dog
   A. Cost of keeping a dog
   B. Time it takes to care for a dog

continued on the next page

As you outline, you may find that you want to rearrange some parts of your presentation. For example, maybe you decide that it would be best to talk about "Things to Consider Before You Adopt a Dog" in the beginning of your presentation. You might also choose to leave some things that you know about your topic out of your presentation. For instance, you might know a lot about how to teach puppies new tricks, but that doesn't belong in a presentation about adopting a dog.

According to RaisingSpot.com, dogs can cost $660 to $5,670 or more in just their first year!

It takes a lot of time to care for a dog. Dogs need regular feeding, exercise, training, and trips to the bathroom. They need even more attention when they are puppies.

There are other ways to organize your information, too. Try writing each fact on a separate note card. Then lay your note cards out on the table in front of you and start to arrange them. You will notice that some note cards seem to go together. For example, a note card about the cost of keeping a dog and another note card about the time it takes to care for a dog might seem related. This shows that you should have a subtopic about things to consider before adopting a dog. From there, you can start to see your subtopics develop, and you can rearrange your note cards into the order that you want to present them to your audience.

# CHAPTER TWO
# Showing Off

⌐ Photographs and other visual aids make
great additions to a presentation.

You know that a good presentation is like telling a good
story. What are some things that can make a story easier
to understand? One good answer is pictures. Oral presentations usually consist of two parts: what you say and
what you show your audience. It is not easy for most people to listen to a presentation without anything to look at.
Good presentations often have visual aids.

There are many different tools that you can use to create interesting and informative visual aids. If you have lots

of time and room for creativity, you might create a play, sing a song, make a video, pass out pamphlets of information, or create a game for the class to play. However, simpler visual aids often help others understand your topic best. That is why many people use a slideshow presentation, using computer programs such as PowerPoint or Keynote, to share visuals with their audience. You create the slideshow on any computer and then project it from a class computer onto a whiteboard or screen for all to see. These slideshow programs offer multiple slides, or screens, to share information in many different forms. You can show important text, images, videos, and more. Let's explore how to best include these elements in your slideshow.

Too many visual aids can distract your audience from the information you are trying to present.

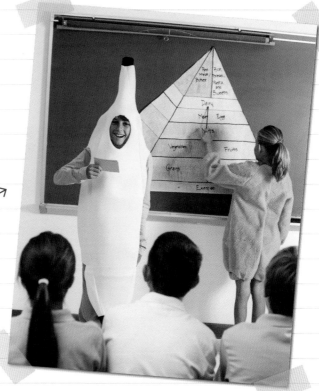

Pay careful attention to the way you organize
information on your slides.

Some of your slides will have text (words or
phrases) written on them to help summarize what you
are saying. Many beginning presenters want to type out
their presentation word for word onto the slides. This
often ends up being a long paragraph, and the presenter
may just read right from the slide. This is very boring
for the audience. Good presenters avoid making this mistake. You can keep notes with extra details you want to
talk about. But not all of this information should appear
on the slides you show the audience.

Try to limit each slide to no more than three or four **bullet points** of information. The "bullets" are small graphics, usually dots, that show different points in a list. Each bullet marks a word, short phrase, or single sentence. Bullet points are quick to read, and they help the audience remember important points in your presentation. For example, a good slide about the history of the Wright brothers' first glider might have the title at the top, followed by three simple bullet points. You will be telling the story out loud, but your slide highlights important facts that you want your audience to remember while you speak. You might create a slide like this:

**WRIGHT BROTHERS' FIRST GLIDER**

• Year—1900
• Kitty Hawk Beach, North Carolina
• Glider was like a kite—held by rope!

It is also important to include images in your presentation. Have you ever heard the saying "A picture is worth a thousand words?" This means that instead of putting up too much text about your topic, you might include an image to show your audience what you are speaking about. Your images should be relevant to your subtopic, meaning they should fit what you are talking about during that part of your presentation. For example, your Wright brothers presentation might include pictures of the brothers when you are introducing them, and pictures of their gliders and aircraft when you talk about how these changed over the years.

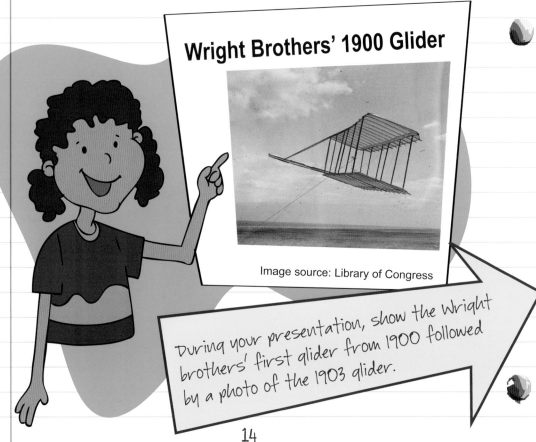

## Wright Brothers' 1900 Glider

Image source: Library of Congress

During your presentation, show the Wright brothers' first glider from 1900 followed by a photo of the 1903 glider.

These images show how the Wright brothers changed the aircraft in just three years. They also show the place where the aircraft was tested—a remote beach. And the black-and-white images hint that this happened long ago. It is helpful to add short captions to your images. This helps the audience understand the images better. For example, a caption for the image of their powered plane might be "1903 Wright Flyer." The caption could be the title of your slide (located at the top of the slide) or it could be text underneath the picture. Either way, make sure it is large enough for your audience to read. You also need to give credit to the place where you got the image. You can do this by including a caption at the bottom of the slide that says something like "Image source: Library of Congress."

**Wright Brothers' 1903 Flyer**

Image source: Library of Congress

Be sure to write a short caption and cite where the picture came from.

Cartoonish clip art does not provide any useful information to your audience.

Some images are not so helpful. Clip art, the cartoon-ish pictures that come with programs like PowerPoint, are often not as useful in a presentation as an image from the actual event. For example, a cartoon picture of a plane flying does not help your audience understand what the Wright brothers' aircraft actually looked like. (The images used on pages 14 and 15 are called primary source documents, which are pictures straight from the actual event!) Animated clip art, or moving images, are not helpful either. More often than not, animations are distracting. If you have a cartoon plane flying around your slide, your audience will spend more time looking at that image than listening to what you are saying.

Remember why you are including these slides with your presentation. The word *aid* means "to help," so think of your visual aids as a way to help others understand your topic better. Your slides must be more than just fun to look at. They must also be informative and helpful.

# TRY THIS!

Some good places to find images include:

http://search.creativecommons.org
Creative Commons' CC Search looks for free media on other Web sites.

www.loc.gov/pictures
The Library of Congress has historical pictures, prints, and documents.

http://pics4learning.com
Pics4Learning is a safe and free image library that's a great resource for teachers and students.

www.clipart.dk.com
DK's picture library site offers thousands of images that are perfect for schoolwork.

http://images.google.com/hosted/life
Google hosts millions of historic photos from Life magazine, from the 1750s to today.

As with any Web search, remember the rules of Internet etiquette and safety. Ask a parent, teacher, or librarian for help if you need it. When you find an image you would like to use, make note of the image's URL so that you can give credit to its owner.

**BE SAFE WHILE ONLINE!**

To get a copy of this activity, visit www.cherrylakepublishing.com/activities.

If you are not sure whether to include a video, ask for opinions from parents, teachers, or friends.

Many audience members love watching video clips during a presentation. Short video clips can enhance your presentation. They give you a short break from speaking and give your audience another way to learn about your topic. You can include, or embed, videos onto your slides. It works a lot like adding images.

Be careful not to use too many video clips! You, not the videos, should be the main presenter of information. Only use short video clips that truly enhance your presentation. This means that the video should show the information better than you could with your words and pictures. After a video clip has played, tell the audience

A good place to begin your search for videos and music is search.creativecommons.org!

what you hoped they learned from the clip. Remember to give credit to the producer of any video you use, just like you would with an image.

Finally, consider including other kinds of graphics, too. You might include a timeline to refer to important events in the history of flight. You might also include charts, graphs, or diagrams, depending on what works best for your topic.

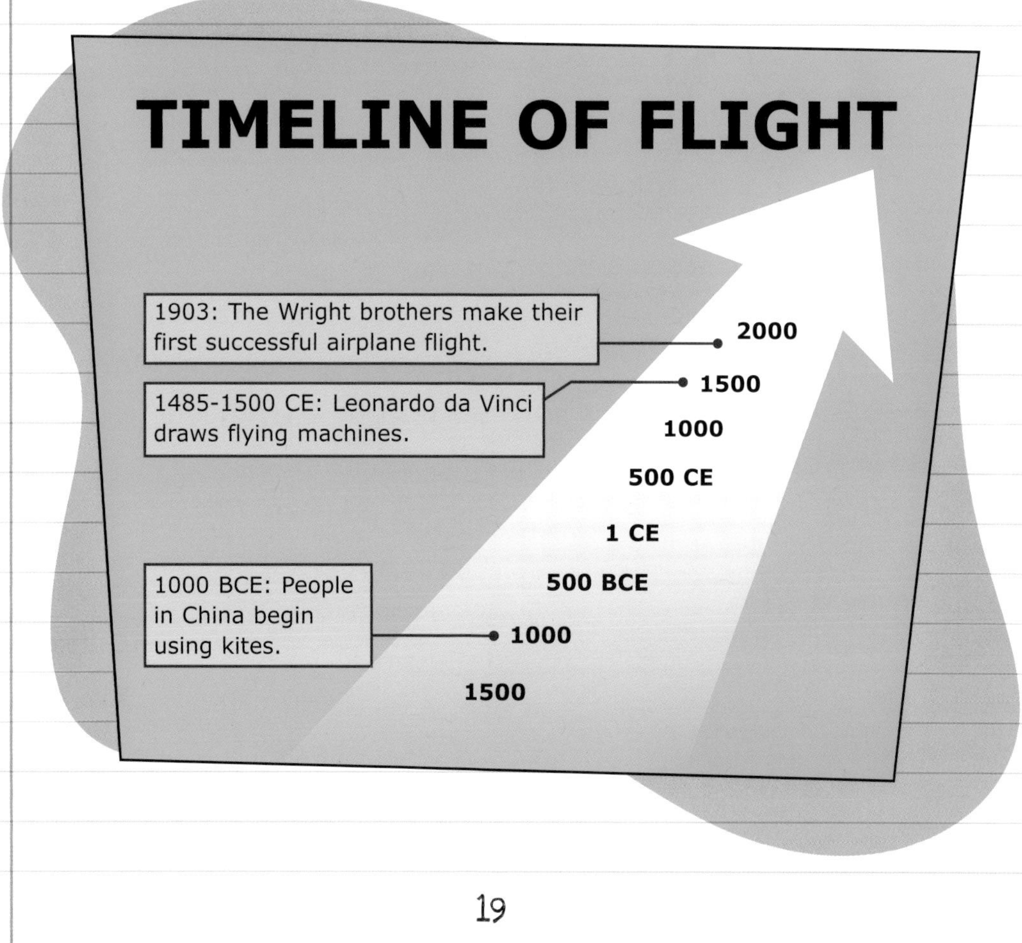

TIMELINE OF FLIGHT
1903: The Wright brothers make their first successful airplane flight.
1485-1500 CE: Leonardo da Vinci draws flying machines.
1000 BCE: People in China begin using kites.
2000
1500
1000
500 CE
1 CE
500 BCE
1000
1500

# TRY THIS!

Sometimes teachers ask you to write a paper and then present your information to the class. This can make it very tempting to simply copy and paste entire paragraphs from your paper onto a slide.

That mistake often leads to one that was mentioned earlier: reading right from the slide! Let's practice avoiding this presentation blunder. Take a look at the paragraph below. Can you turn this paragraph into bullet points for a slide? Can you think of any images that should be included?

Try to buy supplies for your new dog before bringing him home. First, you will need to get food. Be sure that it is the right food for your new dog's age (puppy, adult, or senior). You will also need two bowls for your dog's food and water. Consider where your dog will sleep. You may need a crate and bedding, such as old blankets. You will also need a collar, a leash, and an ID tag. You can sometimes get ID tags at pet stores or at the shelter where you adopt your dog. It's a good idea to bring the leash and collar with you when you adopt your dog.

continued on the next page

Your slide might look something like this:

## Supplies for Your New Dog

- Food
- Collar
- Leash
- ID tag
- 2 bowls (food & water)
- Bedding (old blankets)

How was your slide similar to or different from the one above? Are you surprised by any details that were left off the slide? Why do you think some of the details in the paragraph were left off?

To get a copy of this activity, visit www.cherrylakepublishing.com/activities.

# CHAPTER THREE
# Looking Good

Ask a teacher or a librarian if you are unsure of which fonts you should use.

Deciding what information and images to share in your slideshow is only the first half of creating your visual aid. If you don't consider the design of your slides, your hard work may not pay off.

When you put text, images, and videos on a slide, you have to consider how they will look to your audience. You already know to use bullet points and avoid long sentences and paragraphs, but you should also consider the **font**, or the style and shape of the letters. Computer programs use numbers to tell you how big the text will be. You want the text to be big enough for everyone to read, no matter where they are sitting. Font sizes from 18 to 24 are usually good for presentations.

Keep the font style simple. Avoid fonts that are in cursive or meant to look like handwriting, which can be hard to read. Your best bets are basic fonts, such as Arial, Times New Roman, and Verdana. Use no more than two different fonts in a presentation. You might use one font for slide titles and another for the bullet points. Another benefit of using basic fonts is that they are more likely to stay the same when you bring them to another computer. Many times, you will make a slideshow at home or in a computer lab and then open it on another computer to present in front of the class. The classroom computer might not have some of the strange fonts you included. This will make your words look different than you planned. If you use a basic font, you won't have any surprises!

Contrast makes your
slides easier to read.

**Great
Contrast**

**Good
Contrast**

**Poor
Contrast**

When choosing the color scheme for your slides, it is again best to stay simple. You don't want busy backgrounds with patterns or images. It is best to use a solid color background that provides good **contrast** for your text color. This means that your text color should stick out and be easy to read against your background color. The best combination is a light-colored background with a dark font color. The reverse—a dark background with a light font color—can also work.

Think about the layout of each slide. Don't include too much text or too many images on a single slide. The important text and images will stand out more if there is not a lot of content on the slide. Make titles stand out by putting them in larger fonts and placing them at the top of your slides. Also, keep the most important information near the top and middle of the slides. Remember that your audience in the back of the room might not be able to see the bottom of your slides.

Keep the design of each of your slides consistent. This means that each slide should have the same color scheme and fonts. Design **templates** are included in most slide-show programs, but be careful to choose one that is not distracting and that has good contrast. Make sure that the colors and fonts you choose fit the mood of your presentation. For example, you wouldn't want to use bright or neon colors in a presentation about a very serious or sad topic. Muted colors like a light green or gray would be better for that. Your presentation about the history of flight might benefit from an old-fashioned design scheme. Maybe you want to use a template that looks like it was taken from an old book!

Limit the number of slides that you use. Remember, this is an oral presentation. That means you, not your slides, are the star of your presentation! Try to time your presentation so that there are one or two slides for each minute you are speaking. So, for a five-minute presentation, you might have 5 to 10 slides. Too many slides means you will be rushed, and your audience won't have time to look at each slide.

There are a lot of options in PowerPoint and Keynote that should not be used for a presentation. Music, sound effects, and fancy transitions between slides are often distracting rather than helpful. Your goal is to create a presentation that doesn't need these special effects to capture your audience's attention. Keep people captivated by being a great storyteller with simple but interesting slides.

# TRY THIS!

A poorly designed slideshow can ruin a presentation. Take a look at the slides below and make a list of suggestions or improvements to make each slide better. Check the answers at the end when you are done. How did your suggestions compare?

SAMPLE 1

...around the house. This might also be...
...out your shoes, clothes, and even furnit...
...ing? You want a well-behaved dog that does not jump...
...ing times. You want your dog to listen to you, sit on com...
...walking on a leash. How will you keep your dog in your yard?...
...ard fence, an electric fence, or a chain to keep your dog contained? You...
...your dog to run away and get hurt. These are just some of the things...
...about before adopting your dog.

SAMPLE 3

Image Source: All from OpenClipArt.com

SAMPLE 2

### Adopting After Losing a Pet

- It's okay to grieve for your lost pet
- Remember your pet with a memorial
- Do not try to replace your old pet
- Take time to choose your new pet
- Get to know your new pet for who he is

ANSWERS

1. Use a different color scheme for better contrast, with a solid background. Turn the paragraph into bullet points. Make the font bigger. Make the title more specific to the information being presented on the slide.

2. Have only 1 or 2 pieces of clip art—not 20! Make sure that the clip art fits the topic. Use a more basic font, because cursive can be hard to read.

3. This is a slide about a serious topic, so you should use a more serious font and background. Something more basic would be appropriate. The image should fit the mood, too—maybe a photo of an older dog?

# CHAPTER FOUR
# Be Prepared

With a little practice, you'll be ready to give a perfect presentation.

Once you've created your presentation, it's time to prepare and practice! Rehearse your presentation several times, using your slideshow. Do you need to reorder any of your slides? Make adjustments ahead of time. Look at your visual aids carefully. Check the spelling of all words and read the text on your slides out loud. Does everything make sense? Look at your images. Will they look good blown up on a large screen? Do your videos play when you need them to?

You might have note cards to help you remember what to say during your presentation. There is also a "Notes" section in PowerPoint and Keynote. You can type notes to yourself in that box below each slide. The notes won't show on-screen during the slideshow presentation, but you can print them out and bring them to the presentation. Just make sure that you don't read right from these notes. Use them only to jog your memory!

Practice in front of people who will give you honest feedback, such as family members and friends. Gather as much feedback as possible so that you can make adjustments before you present in front of a big group. Getting critiqued is never easy, but you'll be glad you did this before you get up in front of your whole class. Practice in front of yourself, too! You might do this in front of a mirror, or you might videotape yourself and then watch it with your own critical eye. What do you need to work on? Make sure that you do not say "um" or "like" too much while speaking. Pay attention to your hand gestures, facial expressions, and posture. Practice making eye contact with audience members. Avoid reading from note cards, your paper, or the screen.

Make a list of what you need to bring the day of your presentation. Don't forget to have a backup of your slideshow, perhaps on a flash drive or e-mailed to yourself.

# TRY THIS!

Tell a story you're familiar with. Practice how to stand, use hand gestures, and answer questions about the story. Consider what visual aids you would use while telling the story. Do this in front of a mirror or another person. What did you do well? What needs work to make you the ultimate storyteller?

Practice your presentation in front of a mirror.

Congratulations, Information Explorer! You are on your way to becoming an excellent public speaker. Use these tips, remember to practice, and captivate your audience!

# Glossary

**bullet points (BUL-it POINTS)** small graphics, such as dots, that show different points in a list

**contrast (KAHN-trast)** the difference between two things

**font (FAHNT)** the style of the text you use on a computer

**slideshows (SLIDE-shohz)** series of images or slides that you show to an audience; two popular slideshow programs for computers are Microsoft PowerPoint and Apple Keynote

**subtopics (SUHB-tah-piks)** topics that fall under your main topic; you may have many different subtopics that fit within one main topic

**templates (TEM-plits)** predesigned slides that come built into slideshow programs and can be filled with the user's own information

Don't forget dog treats!

# Find Out More

**BOOKS**

Cornwall, Phyllis. *Put It All Together*. Ann Arbor, MI: Cherry
 Lake Publishing, 2010.

Fontichiaro, Kristin. *Go Straight to the Source*. Ann Arbor, MI:
 Cherry Lake Publishing, 2010.

Rabbat, Suzy. *Find Your Way Online*. Ann Arbor, MI: Cherry
 Lake Publishing, 2010.

**WEB SITES**

**Creative Commons—CC Search**

*http://search.creativecommons.org*

Creative Commons' CC Search looks for free images, videos,
and other media files on the Internet.

**Library of Congress—Prints and Photographs Online Catalog**

*www.loc.gov/pictures*

The Library of Congress has historical pictures, prints, and
documents that you can use for research and including as
visual aids.

**LIFE Photo Archive Hosted by Google**

*http://images.google.com/hosted/life*

Google hosts millions of historic photos from *Life* magazine,
from the 1750s to today.

# Index

About the Author

Ann Truesdell is a school library media specialist and teacher in Michigan. She loves reading, traveling, and spending time with her husband and three children.